PISCES HOROSCOPE
2015

Lisa Lazuli

Lisa Lazuli is the author of the amazon bestseller

HOROSCOPE 2014: ASTROLOGY and NUMEROLOGY HOROSCOPES

ABOUT THE AUTHOR

Lisa Lazuli studied astrology with the Faculty of Astrological Studies in London.

She has practiced since 1999.

Lisa has been a regular guest on BBWM and BBC Shropshire talking about astrology and doing both horoscopes and live readings. She has also made guest appearances on Fox FM, BBC Cambridgeshire, BBC Northamptonshire, BBC Coventry and Warwickshire and US Internet Radio Shows including the Debra Clement Show.

Lisa wrote horoscopes for Asian Woman Magazine.

Now available in eBook and paperback:

TAURUS: Your Day, Your Decan, Your Sign *The most REVEALING book on The Bull yet.* Includes 2015 Predictions.

ARIES HOROSCOPE 2015

TAURUS HOROSCOPE 2015

GEMINI HOROSCOPE 2015

CANCER HOROSCOPE 2015

LEO HOROSCOPE 2015

VIRGO HOROSCOPE 2015

LIBRA HOROSCOPE 2015

SCORPIO HOROSCOPE 2015

SAGITTARIUS HOROSCOPE

CAPRICORN HOROSCOPE 2015

AQUARIUS HOROSCOPE 2015

Lisa Lazuli is also the author of

The mystery/thrillers:

A Sealed Fate

Holly Leaves

Next of Sin

As well as:

Delicious, Nutritious Recipes for the Time and Cash Strapped

Paleo Diet: Get Started, Get Motivated, Feel Great.

99 ACE Places to Promote Your Book

Pressure Cooking Reinvented.

FOREWARD

Dear Reader,

I hope my yearly horoscopes will provide you with some insightful guidance during what is a very tricky time astrologically speaking with the heavy planets i.e. Pluto and Uranus at loggerheads in cardinal signs and Neptune in Pisces calling us all to get in touch with our spiritual side.

I have a conversational style of writing, please excuse any grammatical errors, I write much as I would speak.

As the song goes, "Nobody said it was easy." I know the mass media pump-out shows us plenty about quick fix love, money, fame and success; however, life is a journey filled with challenges and obstacles designed to encourage us to find out what we are made of and who we really are.

Embrace the good and bad and enjoy what is your unique experience.

Be the hero in your own personal life movie and never hide your spotlight.

I must add that the best astrology insights are gained from a unique chart based on your time, date, year and place of birth.

If you would like your natal chart calculated for FREE:

http://lisalazuli.com/2014/06/30/would-you-like-to-know-where-all-your-planets-are-free-natal-chart/

Please join me on Facebook:

https://www.facebook.com/pages/Lisa-Lazuli-Astrologer/192000594298158?ref_hl

Contents

You have a very open attitude this year: you are open to the possibilities of your life and you are also more open emotionally to others and this will enable you to embrace new experiences and new people getting right to the heart of any matter very quickly. The choices will seem limitless although procrastination cab be an issue as with this wide open vista ahead of you it may not be easy to choose. But placing pressure on yourself is not the answer you should allow your instinct to guide you and you should go with the flow of your heart, allowing destiny to make order of the chaos. In fact chaos per se should not concern you as there is more design in what seems to you to be confusion than you realize and things are falling into place quite mystically.

You are highly adaptable this year and your flexibility and able to read situations emotionally can ensure that your timing is excellent and that you take advantage of opportunities as they arise. You are almost chameleon like this year in terms of the way you can act in accordance with each situation you find yourself in. You have a very good feel of the ambient mood be it that of society of within your field of work which enables you to act in subtle yet highly effective ways to capitalize on that mood or prevailing undercurrent. This can be extremely beneficial for writers, artists, journalists, social workers and teachers.

You will find yourself in many new roles this year and it can be an eye opener when you begin to change your perceptions and understanding of others and of your life. Life changes us often without us even noticing and that is what is happening right now; you are becoming more aware more psychic and more in tune with yourself and your world. 2015 is about self-discovery on a deep level – learning more about the person you are as opposed to the job, status and nationality you hold.

You are a very effective mediator this year and may find yourself in supportive, advise giving roles in work and personally – you do however need to think more about boundaries as you have the tendency to be sucked in the tornados of other people's lives and need to know how to step back and reclaim you clam and clarity of mind.

The challenge for Pisces is knowing where you stop and others begin as the desire for all Pisceans is to merge and go with the flow – this year you are encouraged to use your willpower to carve out a more definite structure to your aim and ambitions. You need to think carefully about what it is you need to do in life to feel a sense of personal pride and achievement – do you even know what you want or are you caught up in the expectations of others or the lives of others.

Use your ability to adapt and your powers of perception to seek out avenues which can be highly productive for you. This is a year when you feel great motivation and your energy level is high, You are driven and highly motivated and although choosing a direction or focus will be hard you have a spirit of adventure which will propel you to try a variety of things of which some will play dividends. Do not be deterred by dead ends as the idea this year is to scatter energy and spread your energies over a spectrum so you can follow those which turn out to be fruit and fulfilling.

In life we tend to go through the same cycles again and again until we break that cycle by understand it and addressing the core issue – this is a year when you can begin that journey of breaking old molds and cycles and starting and new script of your life with a new plot and a new theme. How will you break that cycle – total self-honesty and forgiveness. Forgiving those who made mistakes towards you and forgiving yourself.

2015 is much about uncovering the fears and weaknesses which hold us back; but it is not just about the superficial weaknesses we are well away of, it is the deeper emotional drivers of these weaknesses some of which have deep roots in our past. Insecurities, perceived failures, guilt and unresolved issues can all fester in the back of our minds draining us and manifesting as procrastination, bad habits, addictions or compulsions which undermine our will and intent. This year you need to own up to the feelings: examine them and get to a point where you no longer avoid these issue mentally, but you feel comfortable about them to the point where you can reshape the way you think about these issues. We are not defined by failure and weakness is not part of our identity! Failures are a part of life essential for learning and weakness is a symptom not a causal factor. This year you are rediscovering your power to be who you want to be and to direct your life, destiny has been reawakened. Pisces may find that a new person enters their life who acts as a guide, someone who can give you answers and cats a new perceptive on issues and deeper feelings you have. This is certainly a good year to see a counselor to speak about things, however some people stumble upon the answers via meditation or even travel. It is time to discover who you really are and to shake off the attitudes and baggage of life which may have tarnished your shine.

Some Pisces may be dealing with an empty nest syndrome and you may feel conflicted as you release your children into the world either to university or perhaps they are beginning school or getting married and leaving home for good. On one level it may be hard for you to stop worrying and trust in them and on another level you may have to redefine your lace in the world and your role in life – having so much more freedom and time to yourself may be quite intimidating but it is also a wonderful time in your life for rediscovery your own talents and abilities. The theme for Pisces this year is your changing role in life and so even if you do not have children or empty nest for example you may encounter the same issues via other circumstances.

Many Pisces gravitate to the arts world and it is sometimes a cruel one, when we release to the world what we have created we open ourselves up to criticism and comment – the challenge for Pisces is to develop a thick skin and inner resistance to criticism. For all Pisces, the goal is to cultivate a positivity inside and a self-approval where you rate yourself realistically and can distinguish what is constructive comment from what is purely jealousy speaking.

2015 is such a good year for Pisces as you are finding it easier to be assertive and express your independence. You will have many chances this year to make creative changes in your life and to open doors. You will have good relationships with superiors and they can help you to make the most of opportunities that arise. While you have ample energy and plenty of avenues open to you, one problem is a lack of focus – you may scatter your energy and not devise strategies which can help you get where you are going. This is why a mentor or older person who comes into your life can add that structure you need and advise to keep you going as you progress and make decisions.

Pisces who work in organizations (especially those which are socially or charitably orientated) will have the change to rise up the ranks and get enough power to make a big difference especially when you work with communities and political groups.

Feeling good physically this year, your sex life will be full of action. You will be the initiator in giving affection and often in starting off new romances. Pisces have the ability to change negatives patterns in romance and to begin attracting patterns which are positive for you and can help you grow rather than hold you back. In marriages you are able to change the dynamic of your relationship and alter the balance of power so that you have more influence on how you both grow within that relationship.

There is much fun to be had and many exciting trips to go on in 2015. Romances can often start on trip and travel can be very beneficial for existing relationships. It is a very sociable year where will be exposed to different sorts of people who can bring new ideas and often the impetus for change into your life. 2015 is all about new friends and new activities – you are highly pro-active and are grabbing life by the scruff of the neck embracing things you would usually shy away from.

You have a great deal of courage in 2015 and this can allow you to tackle things which you never would have thought you were able to. And the end of the year you will feel a great sense of pride in what you have achieved, not only in terms of career and in concrete terms, but in terms of the way you respect yourself and have improved self-esteem. So this with this ability to draw on reserves of energy, you can direct your life and achieve progress on long held goals as well as feeling more independent and confident in yourself.

LIFE

Stop! Re-think and rethink again. Do not be afraid to go back to the drawing board on ideas and plans as this month you will be challenged to rethink things from a new angle and to take a slightly different direction, if you cannot adapt you thinking you may get stuck in a rut where you cannot make progress. There is a better way and you can see it, but you need to take a few steps back before you can go forward again. Do not be stubborn right now as it will not serve you well.

Start this year with a good clear out – de-clutter and get more systematic. This is a very good time to clear out basements, lofts, storerooms and anywhere you tend to hide old rubbish. In Feng Sui clutter in life leads to clutter in the head – a good tidy up is therapeutic. You should also be careful to either destroy or hide carefully anything which you do not want to be seen – this can be a physical thing like a letter or diary or something you store online. With the internet be very careful about privacy settings and be more au fait about facebook/LinkedIn terms and safeguards.

You may want to start writing a diary right now (bearing the above in mind) or perhaps you diary could be an online blog – either easy you are eager to put thoughts to paper as a way of coming to terms with emotions, conveying fears or getting to grips with repressed emotions. Writing can be very cathartic and it can also be a way of accessing deeper more complex emotional issues which defy logic – you may write prose, poetry or music to gain these benefits. You may even find that writing down pro and con lists can help you clarify a situation. It may be useful if you are writing a diary to re-read things a week or so later to gauge how you thinking may have changed and you can analyze why.

This is a very good time to begin any therapy ie grief/debt/marriage/phobia counselling, psychology, aptitude tests etc as you are in tune with your deeper self and any psychometric analysis can be more helpful than usual in unpicking and deciphering emotions.

LOVE

Workplace romances may start suddenly this month; it may not be someone in your office but perhaps someone from you company you meet on a business trip or someone who is also an expert in your field or in the same career or perhaps someone in the same company but another division. There is a sense of distance here and so while you may meet in the course of work, you will not most probably be seeing each other every day at work which is a far better situation. This new relationship will get off the ground very quickly and you will find that you are able to open up about subjects close to your heart. You may have to try hard to reign in your feelings and you will realize that you heart had run off very quickly and you head has yet to catch up. You should enjoy the relationship while not putting everything on the line – retain a small amount of emotional aloofness and do not overlook anything about the other person which could later become significant to you.

Marriages and established relationships will fare well this month with a good vibe pervading your communications and affections. You are both forgiving and fun loving which is an ideal cocktail for love. There will be a feeling in all relationships new and old of a fresh new start – like you are moving forward. Often relationships become stagnant and stale, but right now you are excited about life with your partner and are in love again and it's a good feeling.

CAREER

It may be time to throw out old formulas and action plans even if they have served you well in the past; think of new approaches and be bold in the way you communicate with customers or clients.

Dealing with international clients or customers is a feature of this month, although issues to do with customs and excise, shipping delays or security issues can waste your time and cause frustration. Having appropriate insurance is a must, so research that well. Do your homework and make you import tax calculations thoroughly to avoid going over budget.

Health and safety law may become an important issue for you or your business and whether you are claiming or you are the employer, you will need to learn more about relevant laws or compensation claims. It is important for those who are not self-employed to be more aware of your rights as an employee especially when it comes to health insurance and benefits, sick pay and sick leave.

Although no one is overjoyed to be back at work in January, there is a feel good factor and a fun vibe at work right now and camaraderie is great. If you are starting a new job for the new year, things are looking fabulous and you will fit in and make new friends fast.

LIFE

This month misplaces expectation can cause delays and disappointment, but they can also be quickly rectified. You may find that one door closed, but another door you never even anticipated opens and so it is a month of unexpected opportunities and pleasant reversals of fortune.

This is a very powerful month for getting your own way – you are both diplomatic and assertive and while you come across as accommodating you are still focused on getting what you want and need from any situation. You are in a pro-active frame of mind and you feel good about yourself. This is a month of being self-centered and going after things that will make you happy. It is very important to prioritize, organize and then get suck in, you motivation level is high but to make the most of it you will need to have an outline to work to. Make sure you know what your objectives are as seeing progress is very important to you right now, but you cannot measure progress against something vague so set yourself goals and targets.

A very sociable month with parties and events to go to and since you are feeling outgoing and confident you can make the most of these events for networking and for spotting potential ne love interests what with it being Valentine's Day this month.

Sometimes in life we do not make the most of ourselves and we do not grab every opportunity as we feel in some way undeserving – this is a month to say, "I want it and I deserve it!" Drop any thoughts that you do not deserve something and do not allow yourself to be put in the corner.

LOVE

A lover from the past may resurface in your life leading to some mixed emotions and even an awkward moment in your current relationship. If you are single you may meet unexpectedly with a lover from the past: perhaps it was the one that got away or someone you parted on bad terms with. You should not try and revisit this relationship, you should rather use it as an opportunity to resolve it in your mind. It may be that meeting up again after a long time with someone you once loved will confirm to you that that person was indeed no good for you and it would never have worked.

If you are married this is also a time when events will arise that will enable you to set issues with a former boyfriend/girlfriend to bed. This is a period of closure and will not lead to the reawakening of feelings for that person.

There is a strong feeling of re-committing to your spouse or long term partner this month with a renewed affection and also sexual arousal. What you need to do right now is let love flow and stop stipulating how things should be and what course love should follow – allow yourself to be spontaneous in love and to revel in the uniqueness and quirkiness of you relationships instead of trying to match up with what you perceive others have or other's do. Appreciate the unique qualities of your relationship and how that makes you feel, rather than focusing on unrealistic templates of so called perfect relationships.

CAREER

Analysis and piecing information together will come easily to you this month and things will really click – so any mental task or number crunching which has been getting you done will fall into place. You may have been on the verge of hiring someone to help you and explain something to you, but now you see it clearly and can make your own choices without external input.

This month if you want a job done properly you must do it yourself; you cannot fully rely on others and delegating with be tricky. It is also better for you to do tasks yourself rather than letting others do it or hiring someone to do it as you need your finger firmly on the pulse and the only way to do that is to be involved. Work hard to understand fully the aspects of your work which are most important so that you can keep an eye on things – for example it's easy to delegate the financial side of a business to an accountant and they have no more to do with it than necessary, however the lesson this month is not to rely on others to such a degree that you must trust them completely. Make sure you look everything over when you delegate and be critical of anyone who does anything on your behalf.

An excellent month for selling or for coordinating a presentation at a trade fair or market. You can deal with people with great aplomb and charm right now, this will help you nail deals.

LIFE

This is a very important month for Pisces as the solar eclipse is giving you a boost of energy and personal power. This is a wonderful time to start new projects and initiate new activities which can take your life in an exciting new direction. This is also a time of health turnabouts – take your health in hand and look into new diets, fitness regimes or lifestyles that can improve your energy, the way you feel about yourself and your vitality. I know we often do what I said in the last paragraph and fail, but this time you can succeed and really make a difference to your mental and physical states becoming more motivated and happier too.

This is a time when you feel a greater sense of self and of the power you have to direct your life – it is a time of decisions and of taking the reins into your hands. It is also a phase in your life when by being more assertive and insistent on following your callings you can develop better inter personal relationships. Passive aggression is not an issue right now as you feel able to express yourself and take center stage in your life, not playing second fiddle to any person.

You are able to shine a spotlight on any aspect of your life that you feel needs change or more focus and by working on this aspect of life you can strengthen your personality and project yourself into the world with more confidence. March is all about drawing on inspiration from within and realizing what resilience and power you have deep inside.

LOVE

Love and relationships can really succeed and move to more fulfilling level of communication and intimacy due to the strength and self-knowledge you are gaining as a person. We all know that learning to love yourself is the greatest love of all and yet we all often seek the validation of another person in terms of love and marriage in order to convince ourselves that we are lovable.

You are surer of what you want and that means you are sending out direct messages to your partner which are easy for him/her to interpret. Communication is excellent and you can diplomatically broach sensitive subjects and get them into the open and cleared up. As you are in a conciliatory mood you will find it easy to put aside differences and focus on common ground.

This is not a month of putting yourself second, it is more a time when you can cooperate and negotiate to get more of what you want out of the relationship.

New relationships are flourishing right now and Pisces are not holding back, while you are sometimes shy in romance, at the moment you are sure of what your heart is telling you and ready to go with it, even making the first move if required.

CAREER

This month is very lucrative for those of you who have unusual talents or who have the courage to go with an off the wall or unorthodox idea – if you have had an idea in mind, do not let convention and any conservative thoughts from those around you hold you back. This is a time when something outlandish can come off and where lateral thinking must be applied.

It can be an up and down month for finances and so do not commit to a large outgoings beforehand if you can help it – keep financially flexible in March. This is a good month to get some advice on financial planning – try and free up resources, adjust gearing or change the way you make pension payments or make us of tax credits. A certain scattiness over the finer points of you finances could be losing you money whether you are self-employed or an employee so get on top of this – your partner may be able to help if they are financially minded.

Financial independence is very important to you and so if you are a student; you may take a part time job to get more independence from your parents; if you are a stay at home mom you may decide to go back to work or you may leave your current job for something that offers more prospects financially or benefits. Organizing your finances both personal and business is vital now wo that you can pay down debt as a priority to gain more financial flexibility as the year goes on.

LIFE

Moderation is the key this month: you are highly motivated and enthusiastic and yet you may attempt too much to prove something to yourself. It is a time when you are driven to take chances and you want to challenge yourself, but you are not always wise in the way in which you go about this. Advice can be very useful, but you need to know which advice is helpful and which advice is just a pessimist who envies your optimism talking. Did you ever hear, "I only want what is best for you,"? Never believe this as only you know what is best for you and to find your own destiny you must follow your heart, however this month you are not seeing things in sharp perspective and you may be want to head the advice of those you genuinely trust and whom have given you wise advice in the past. Select you advisors with care.

You are very competitive and physically vital this month and so this is an ideal time to train for something or undertake a sporting challenge. If you have a deadline or are working hard to complete on a goal this is a month when you can make great strides as you are highly productive and capable of directing your energy and that of others towards the end goal. You have the ability to be very motivating and an encouraging to others.

This is another good month for health and your body will feel stronger. An inner optimism as well as a burst of energy can help you overcome physical problems. It is important to recognize the link between mind and body and how much your mental attitude impacts on your health and ability to recover from illnesses. A stronger mental attitude may be what you need to work on rather than your body – this can be in terms of fitness or indeed recovery from illness. Do not underestimate the holistic nature of health – it is possible that you have become too focused on one element ie fitness or diet or medicating ate the expense of the other elements.

Be more balanced in your approach and pay attention to mind, body and soul.

LOVE

A need for peace and quite this month is countered by a need to take a firm stand on every day matters. Yes, Pisces are easy going and you like to be hands off in terms of mundane everyday affairs, but this month you can be rather irritated and feel as if you do not do something no one else will. You may have to initiate some strongly worded discussions in order to set the record straight and make sure your partner respects both you and the household rules. Love is great, but respect is pretty crucial as well and this month is about you getting that respect and about making sure that you are not in a double standards relationships.

Issues that may arise could be to do with the time you spend with your family/friends relative to your partners or it may be to do you your opinions be heard and taken more seriously or perhaps it is the way you spend your time. You need to ensure there is more balance and that your ideas, family, friends and opinions are not always taking a back seat. These issues should be easily resolved, bit must not be neglected.

April is also a wonderful time to spend together as a family and you may undertake home decorating or improvements which make your home more comfortable, cozy and reflective of you as a couple.

A fun month for single Pisces as you are mingling and meeting many new people – you may meet up with someone from you past and realize there is a connection you may want to explore.

CAREER

You are mentally sharp and highly resourceful right now. You can do well in any pressure situations this month ie exams, high power meetings, nailing deals, stock market trades. It is a month of high intensity where you will sometimes rely on gut feel to make a decision. You can be very effective and you will excel.

Those who work in medical fields especially will find this a month of fast paced activity and a steep learning curve, you are able to deal with long shifts and have good concentration.

In any career you should not let this month go by without tackling something – use the energy you have to make an impact and excel at what you do. You may try and learn some new technique or about some new software or perhaps take a crash course in a new language – whatever you decide to do, make a pro-active choice for the better and get stuck in.

In creative careers stand behind your choices and stick with your decisions – defend you way of doing things and have total faith in yourself. Do not give up or give in!

LIFE

You may surprise yourself this month in terms your emotional response to people especially in the family environment; sometimes an emotion or feeling can jump out of nowhere and take hold of you. Often you may feel as if you do not even know yourself. It may be that you finally begin to acknowledge of something in your past has affected you: by dwelling on this issue you may get a better understanding on why it may have happened and perhaps you will be able to put a new more positive spin on it.

You are highly influenced by the undercurrents within your home and if there is a negative atmosphere it is best for you to get away from that as other people's negative emotions are especially toxic for you. Cleanse your aura often by showering and bathing and then get to a place where you can feel safe and generate some positivity. If you are feeling blue right now; it may be down to you absorbing someone else's bad vibes, more that something you are generating. Pisces are very porous emotionally and you can be highly sensitive to the prevailing mood – that is why this month especially you need to be with people who ooze positive emotions.

You may have relations staying over with you in May and you will find this rather disruptive to your own routines. There is a certain chaotic element to your home life in May and you will have to be flexible and make some sacrifices in terms of your personal space. You have a feeling of being invaded right now and you need to withdraw to a place (either a physical or a mental space via meditation) where you can gain some balance and get your head cleared.

You can be rather scatty this month and so it is not a good time to make decision of a financial or technical nature.

LOVE

Relationships are intense this month whether they are new or established and there can be a subtle battled of wills. You may not actually argue but something is simmering below the surface and it may be hard for you to broach the issue as you may think that you perhaps are imagining something.

You are picking up signals and yet your partner may deny that there is anything wrong – perhaps they are carrying something which they are unwilling to talk about but which you can sense. This is a month when deep seated issues in the relationship will make life awkward and an unwillingness by your partner to talk can frustrate you.

The sex can potentially be very good and yet the underlying emotions are not loving. It is a complex and confusing month for relationships when deep seated issues can act like dead holly leaves which continue to prick. Often the cause of relationship difficulty this month is beyond your control and may even lie in the distant past – the best way to deal with problems is by not trying to control things or delve too deeply into them. Calmness, understanding and patience is the anecdote for all relationships in May. Sometimes we have to have our secrets and our silences and we must let others have them too.

WORK

This is a wonderful month for writers and journalists as you will find a wealth of material at your fingertips – you are highly tuned in right now and able to touch a nerve with your writing, which is just what good writing should do. This is also a wonderful month for actors as you have the ability to step into a character and feel the emotions of that character as your own. This month will be very fruitful for Pisces who conduct research or whose field of study is linked to history or pharmacy.

May is a highly productive month in any career where a sense of timing is important or where your ability to empathize or understand a client is essential. You are operating at a highly psychic level and although it may not be straightforward to interpret to signs you are getting, with a little logic added on you will find that you can come up with amazing solutions. This ability can be especially helpful in careers where you diagnose or where you use your hands to help people to make physical recoveries ie physiotherapist, occupational therapy, chiropractors, Osteopaths etc.

Those who write about or teach creative subjects or literature – anything where an intuitive rather than logical understanding is essential. You have an excellent ability to convey complex issues.

May is not an ideal month to deal with property and real estate – avoid closing deals or making offers as there may be hidden problems or issues that only come to light after the purchase.

LIFE

June is an ideal time to do a little audit of where you are in terms of your goals for the year and you should make new plans and strategies based on how things are going to ensure you stay on track. Family matter are very important right now and family events may bring you into contact with family member you have not seen for years. You may renew a friendship with a cousin or another relations who you had lost touch with.

This may be the month you move to a new residence; last month was not a good time to plan a house move but this is a much better month to move or sign a new agreement on a lease. A move will be an excellent motivation to get rid of old junk and things from the past which no longer have any meaning. Even if you are not moving this is an ideal time to clear out places in your home with are cluttered and to get on top of paperwork. Take time to finish things off before you start new projects and make sure that you are diligent in the way you tie up loose ends.

During this month you may begin to examine triggers ie things which set off certain reactions within you. This month and this year especially, you need to realize that what you think of you is what really matters and not what others think or say about you is irrelevant if those people are your parents– reverse mental conditioning from childhood and reprogram yourself to seek happiness for yourself and not live life for the sake of other's needs and values. This year in an important one of self-discovery and life path discovery. You are glimpsing your own unique destiny as distinct from what you may have been conditioned to want or strive for.

LOVE

A month of promise for love relationships.

Your spouse or partner can help bring laughter and adventure into your life right now. You may travel long distance due to your partners work or to because your partner is visiting his family who live abroad. In some cases Pisces may move away from their home town or home country in order to start a new life with their partner. Even in new relationships Pisces will suddenly be exposed to new horizons and perhaps even some challenging yet exciting circumstances. You may have to fend off skepticism but you are ready to follow your heart.

Pisces are benefitting from an open hearted attitude which is enabling you to share more easily and open up in a manner which help your partner gain an understanding of your hopes and aspirations. Our hopes often reflect the best in us and yet a need for stability can perhaps bring out the worst; however this month you are driven by the highest values and ethics and you will really achieve respect from your partner.

New relationships can be very successful right now as you have so much energy to give and you are devoid of cynicism, seeing only the best and bringing out the best in others.

Resist parental interference in your love life and remember that their advice may not be helpful or may be driven by motives you do not understand.

CAREER

This month you will have to take a long hard look at plans and determine which are simply not practically possible at the moment and set them aside for another time. Practical considerations especially financial ones must take precedence of pet projects and issued which may be close to your heart.

This month most school and universities in the Northern Hemisphere have exams and close for summer and this period is really very fortunate time for all Pisces who are studying or taking exams as your concentration and ability to write coherently and with logic is enhanced. Clarity of mind will aid all those who study in achieving good results which they are proud of.

June is also a perfect month for those working toward deadlines and under pressure as you can work with speed and accuracy and achieve great productivity and even promotion of recognition. Keeping to rules and following protocols is very important in all careers; it is not about sucking up to your superiors but showing respect for the way they do things can score you more points that trying to show that your way is better.

In all jobs, stick to the straight and narrow and err on the side of caution – be thorough and make sure you keep good records and time sheets as a small detail may end up being more important than you think.

LIFE

You are very busy right now at work and you are enjoying what you are doing as your work right now seems to have a broader scope: in terms of meeting people and life experience. Travel in connection with work is a very big possibility and you may also be able to mix a fair amount of pleasure with your work trips.

Further education and study may play a big role in your life and it may be sponsored by your employer or it may be something you undertake with the aim of getting a new position at work which with give you more freedom and provide you better prospects.

Health is something which can easily be overlooked in July and excess in all forms can lead to some problems: not only excess of food and alcohol but even an excess of supplements or too strict an adherence to a dietary plan. Be middle of the road when it comes to health and do not veer onto the periphery of normality in your pursuit of fitness or slimness.

Take a cautious approach to legal dealings which begin now and do not rush them, take you time to become totally au fait with the terms and conditions as ignoring something vital now could have quite a disruptive impact on your life later down the line. If you do need to initiate some legal proceedings against someone, now is a very good time as you can probably get the matter resolved by Christmas.

There is much pride taken in what you do right now and offering service to others (ie friends, family or even strangers) in need can bring you a sense of personal pride. While it is not good to become obsessed; this month you may spend a vast amount of time on a personal project making sure it is 100% to your satisfaction and this can be extremely rewarding.

LOVE

This is one of those months when relationships need work – you will need to be patient and persevering to make sure your love life runs smoothly and events, especially those to do with in laws and your work will challenge the harmony and force you to make concessions. Small and larger problems can be thrust into focus and must be discussed calmly, not only during arguments.

You may have to make choices in love which are not straightforward and you may end up doing things which you later find hard to defend. It is a tough month to know how to make the best of things and how to keep everyone happy. It's important to remember right now that you cannot please all the people all the time and to a large degree others are responsible for their own happiness and well-being and it is not up to you to be your partner's mother. This month, make sure you do not take all the responsibility or blame for how things are going in the relationship – you partner needs to pull themselves together and not rely so much on you to do the bending and adapting.

This is a month when you need a rebalancing within your love relationships – an assessment of the give and take and how much there is of each. It is a very good time to take a step back and say, "OK, what is really going on here?" If you can look at yourselves in perspective and see the good, the bad and the problems, you can make adjustments now which can really improve things in the coming months.

In new relationships Pisces need to be more honest with themselves about where and how the new love interest is going and if it has potential.

CAREER

You are enjoying work right now partly due to enhanced rapport with colleagues and co-workers and the increased amount of more interesting work you are doing. You work load may well increase but you are finding the work stimulating and you are improving your skills at the same time. You may find that you are asked to train up new staff or you may contribute to a training manual of professional journal.

If you are in a profession or an expert in a field you may well get noticed this month and you may be called upon to talk on radio or contribute to a publication. This is a great time to publish a book on a technical subject you know much about.

Those of you in service industries will find that business is going very well. You may begin to offer your services to a new clientele either geographically or culturally.

This is an excellent month for Pisces who are seeking to change employment in order to find better working conditions or those who are seeking employment as fortune is with you. It is a time of opportunity within career. If you are looking for work look within the legal fields, police work, the courts, printing, tourism or promotions or even the army.

A once in a lifetime opportunity may come to you via work this month.

Someone once said, "Advice is useless, that's why it's free!" However this month advice from someone can really be very useful. If you are having any problems making a decision then a second unbiased or even professional opinion can be very helpful. This is a month when you may feel bombarded with conflicting information and you may not be able to decide what or who to believe; that is a why an impartial third person could clarify issues for you.

This is also a good time to clear up matters in your own mind – if there is something you should have done before or need to do in order to get something off your mind or off your conscience you should take steps now to put that matter to bed. This is a month to make sure bygones are bygones and make peace with others and also with yourself.

Sometimes are thoughts are our worst enemy and we can let negative thoughts run out of control to the point where we are just not being rational and often things are never as bad as we imagined – this month face up to those things you have been avoiding they will be nowhere near as bad as you had imagined and you will feel as if there is a load off you mind when you have addressed these issues.

Often it can be harder to quieten our own nagging voices of criticism than to deal with other peoples; this month you will find other people very helpful and supportive to you emotionally and in terms of your goals – you must however deal with your own doubts by replacing them with pro-active encouraging thoughts.

LOVE

You should not mix love and the office this month. Whether you are single or in a relationship keep flirting in work situations to minimum as it can become complicated and uncomfortable. There is a desire to be impulsive in love, but you should think twice as your judgment is a little cloudy this month and situations can turn out very differently than expected.

Love relationships that are well established and stable will do very well this month; with things going smoothly but with just a little extra zing to make the days sparkle. This is a time when consistency pays off and provides that security and reassurance you need. If your partner is erratic and moody right now that can rub off on you, making you feel very uneasy. Try to create as much stability and predictability in love as you can this month as that will help you both to feel at ease. If your partner is upset, you should support him/her without allowing yourself to become emotionally involved – be loving but give the advice he/she needs to hear rather than telling him/her what he/she wants to hear. It may be time for some tough love, do not indulge your partner's self pity.

In general you are optimistic about relationships right now and are taking a positive and forward looking approach, excited about what the rest of the year may hold. Your strong and positive attitude together with a practical approach will help keep all relationships on an even keel.

CAREER

If you work in the arts and creative fields this can be a month when criticism and having to make changes and adjustments is hard to swallow. You may have to bite your tongue and commit yourself to editing, cutting and redoing work. You will in the process find things which can be improved and you will end up with an even better result.

In business this marks a month when going into partnership or a joint venture can be an excellent idea to expand your business or your career prospects. Pisces enjoy working with people especially people who have a strong feel for the financial and management side.

Pisces are often less focused and can be scatty and so a partnership can allow Pisces the freedom to express their creative and inspirational side without becoming bogged down with managerial details. It is likely that you will go into partnership with someone who is older or more established and who already has access to channels or networks which can help the business get off the ground.

Financially this can be an onerous month with bills to pay or insurance premiums to renegotiate, so do not undertake any big expenditure. Watch out for changes in the terms and conditions of loans or your repayment schedules.

Pisces should make sure their tax paperwork is being kept up to date and all your info is backed up as problems that arise now can make filing your return more complicated.

A very interesting and also informative month for Pisces who are psychologists, counselors or even psychic and those who use esoteric/new age means to help people – you can make progress in increasing your understanding and developing your own practical techniques and systems to help others. You may develop a new psychometric test, therapeutic technique or learning program.

LIFE

This is a month full of fun, novelty and excitement. You will be meeting new people and trying new things.

This is also a month of talents rediscovered! You may have a skill or an ability which you have not used for ages, but this month events may encourage you to start thinking about how you can use that talent again. It's not just about talent it's about rediscovering an activity which you really enjoyed which allowed you to feel good about yourself.

The pace of September is fast and events can be quite random, but the break in routine is very exciting and spontaneous events and parties will add much excitement to life. Pisces are not always pro-active, you like to go with the flow, however this year you have felt able to strike out and act in a way in which to direct your life and take control. This month it is not so much moving in a definite direction or even with a plan, it is about expressing yourself and trying new things which have the potential to change your life. Often in life we do not need a map with all the details filled in, it is enough to make the first step and let the details fall into place after that.

The feeling of creating possibilities and enjoying the unexpected will reinvigorate you this month. You have an abundance of energy and will not be easily about to settle to routines and mundane work – it's a great month for unexpected get togethers and for going to launches and to hot new places in town.

Take chances this month and follow your heart. Enjoy being spur of the moment and do not hold back.

LOVE

This is the best month of the year for single Pisces to meet a new lover and start new relationships. You are feeling bold and confident and have a sparkling quality about yourself that is highly attractive. Pisces are known for their sense of humor and you are extremely witty and entertaining at the moment. Cupid could strike at any time and you may fall in love completely unexpectedly. Do not expect your love life to follow a conventional form however as this relationship will be unorthodox yet very rewarding.

This is also a very positive month for all alternative relationships and you can gain acceptance from peers and family. Being you and being true to you is so vital right now and you have the courage to fly in the face of any criticism – it's about you and doing it your way.

Established relationships and marriages can be very exciting right now as new friends or a financial windfall can help you both the experience life in a different way. You are both highly energetic and open to possibilities right now and this is the perfect environment for reawakening fun, passion and conversation in relationships.

An adventurous and curious spirit will help love relationships to go extremely well when it comes to both sex and conversation. You can have many laughs together this month.

CAREER

This month is highly lucrative for graphic designers, software designers, music production (arrangement and composition), modern art and inventors. You can have great success marketing anything with has a novelty factor! It is all about being trendy, innovative and ground breaking and so you should strive in your career or business to be original and even 'out there' in terms of products and the way you tackle problems.

This is a fortuitous month to launch a new product, a book or a production. This is also a highly productive month for those in emerging industries.

Try and arrange your work so that you are flexible this month and can take advantage of sudden money making opportunities. This may be a great time to start a new business or turn a hobby into a money making opportunity. If are self-employed look to make more use of under used assets or reorganize your finances to free up cash.

The wider economy can have an impact on your life and your finances this month – however if you are imaginative and courageous there can be an opportunity to make money. Pisces in the stock market or investment world can use foresight of business trends to make money out of a chaotic stock and share movements this month.

LIFE

You may have to defend and fight for your values this month – issues of principle are on the line and you will not want to back down although you will have to make some compromises. Sharing with others can cause you some anxiety and you will have to endure a degree of imposition on your territory in some way.

You can be rather sentimental this month; you will cling to relics of the past which perhaps you should let go of and yet you will resist changes especially if they are forced on you. It can be a challenge to move forward and forsake things from the past: you make also have to accept that some of your ideas about how you want to live your life need to adapt. You need to loosen you grasp on anything which is holding you back from growth. Sometimes we sacrifice excitement and adventure in our lives for security and this can lead us into a rut which can be rather cosy and welcoming if not passive and boring. This month you are going to be challenged to sacrifice some of that safety and security in order to broaden your horizons – you need to allow yourself to be taken out of both your mental, emotional and physical comfort levels so that your life can become more dynamic.

One problem of this month is over thinking and over analyzing people and situations – perhaps you are keen to extract explanation where there is none or meaning from what could just be random comments.

If purchasing or leasing property make sure you are aware of any right of way or other rights pertaining to that property which may affect how you are able to use it.

LOVE

Clashing ideas about how to raise children and spend the joint finances can cause some disharmony and you may have to give way and yield to what may be a more pragmatic approach by your partner. There is a string urge to do it your way and reject input, but you can gain so much more by working with your partner instead of pulling against him/her. This month teamwork in partnerships is very important, set your differences aside and concentrate on what you can achieve and the goal you are striving for as the goal is bigger than the trivial differences which divide you although it can take a while to see that.

This is a very good month for sexual renewal and an improvement in your sexual relations, however you must learn to switch off and give sex your full attention – intimacy is impossible if your mind is elsewhere and so worries and concerns about work etc must be left outside the bedroom so that you sex life can be the fulfilling bubble of escapism that it should be.

This is a month when Pisces in new relationships may move in together and there may conflict regarding the new living arrangements in keeping with this month general theme of issues to do with property ownership and rights over property.

CAREER

Communication within you work is a major part of this month and you will spend much time writing, re-writing and making calls. You may have to make a speech or prepare extensively for a presentation or sales pitch. On a deeper level this month you may be inspired to give a voice to someone who does not have one: this can mean giving a voice to a child who is abused, telling the story of someone who has passed one or getting justice for a vulnerable group whom society has neglected. You have the power this October to bring the world's attention to something you care about, to something which has meaning to you. You can do this for your business or to promote a wider concern of yours.

For Pisceans who work in social work, psychology or even law enforcement it is a challenge for you to put what you intuitively understand into words which can be documented.

Be careful when you make use of material which is subject to intellectual property rights and ensure anything you publish is properly copyrighted. Jointly owned rights or jointly owned property can be the source of disputed this month and during the next few months so make sure you are well aware of your own rights and of the law.

LIFE

You may get a little down on yourself this month and feelings of despair and inadequacy may dog you. However, you are very idealistic right now and you may have been somewhat unrealistic and so instead of feeling downhearted you need a more down to earth appraisal of how things are going, after which you will see they are not so bad at all.

This month you are inclined to be very distracted and dreamy, it is not such a good month to deal with practical matters, it is however a wonderful month to deal with subjects which require imagination, inspiration and insight. You may also be drive to travel in order to volunteer or sacrifice your time for those who are in desperate need. You have a very strong desire to reach out to others.

You are extremely imaginative and creative right now, you can excel in any field where a flow of ideas or brainstorming is required. November is a superb time for artists, poets, photographers, designers or writers. Photographers or cinematographers can create images more powerful than words.

This is also a wonderful time for those of you who teach – you have the ability to inspire enthusiasm and interest and to put across complex issues. In whatever you do right now you are bringing a massive amount of emotional intelligence to bear in how you handle people and situations, you have an uncanny insight which can allow you to understand on a level few others can. You have the ability to reach people either on a personal level or via your art form in a way that can transform or touch a life. Pisces live and feel on a higher spiritual level and this month you can convey your deepest feelings in a way that is transformative for you and enlightening for others.

There may be a desire to take risks just for the thrill; try and avoid this avenue and express yourself via art, music or in a positive way socially.

LOVE

This month it is very important for Pisces women to examine how their attitude to and relationship with their father is affecting their love relationships. It is also an issue for gay men to consider. How did you father make you feel about your identity and your independence? If your father was very distant are you attracting me who are also distant and vague? Was your father domineering and are you now attracting men who are controlling and manipulative. It is a good time to re-examine how much of your relationship with your father influences how you behave with or experience your partner now. Issues this month with your father or a father figure will bring you some perspective on how your father either helped or hindered your emotional development and how any scars from childhood negatively impact on your love life now.

This is a month where you will be confronted with patterns which you repeat unconsciously especially in matters to do with men. Issues to do with co-dependency and your own insecurity come to the fore. You have the ability right now to break these patterns and establish new patterns where your inner security and self-esteem starts with you and inside you is independent of anyone else and their behavior towards you. Don't wait for a hero to save you, be your own hero and save yourself.

For men as well as women, analyze how much your father's approval or lack of it affected you – think about the wounds you still have from the way he acted or omitted to act. It is time to heal those wounds with a positive self-love and self-forgiveness. Do not try and use you love life as a sticking plaster; work on healing the wounds and casting away the negative reflexes you have in your current relationships stemming from father-issues.

CAREER

A desire to change the world and to see the bigger picture is inspiring Pisces right now. If you work in an office, in admin or in finance, you may not be able to change the world, however your kindness and concern for those you work with and your ability to bring a positive vibe to the office can make a big difference to everyone. You may decide to get everyone at work involved in a sponsored drive to raise money for a cause you believe in or you may use the platform you have via your work to raise awareness about an illness of disease.

Pisces are the ideas-people in any work situation this month and can provide both the creative and emotional inspiration needed. Pisces are not great with details and can be rather lax over procedural issues; so perhaps delegate these out or get someone to check over your work for errors.

A teacher or mentor may come into your life right now and take you under their wing helping you to learn and progress in your career or helping you into a new career.

Health and healing are a massive theme in November and this is an excellent month for any Pisces who is embarking on a career in the medical fields either alternate, traditional or pharmaceutical and it is also a time when those already in these fields can make their mark and have a big impact on the life of their patients. Pisces looking for work or deciding what to study should seriously consider the health and healing fields.

This is an excellent time to write or publish a book on diet, health, psychology, spirituality or mind power. This month is also a very powerful one for those involved in spiritual teaching, religion or giving guidance/assistance to groups ie AA, victims of abuse, drug abuse support etc.

LIFE

This can be a rather frustrating month and you must be patient and organized in order to achieve what you aim to. More haste less speed is the motto. Be diligent and work consistency towards your end of year goals and tie things up properly. This is not the the time to rush or force issues; things must be worked through and it will take as long as it takes. Results can be achieved but not instantly. Hard work and effort will pay dividends, taking short cuts will end up costing you and your reputation.

You will reflect on your goals and how you ambitions and aims changed this year to reflect the evolution in your own personality; you must plan on how to take all your initiative forward, do not let things slip in 2016. It is also a time to make fun goals to strive for next year ie events to look forward to and reward yourself with.

Take advantage of this time of year to renew contacts with friends and your extended family - remember the importance of your wider support network and make sure you thank them and wish them for the New Year. You will be in increased contact with young people this month and they will help you get in touch with the child within – which can teach you something about a part of you which you may have lost along life's long and winding road.

LOVE

You are in an excitable mood and looking forward to Christmas. December is a very good month for new and older relationships and relations with he in laws should be running smoothly too.

Sexually this month can be rather experimental with a degree of novelty. Pisces men are quite assertive and amorous in terms of their advances and if you are with a Pisces man, get ready for some passion.

A philosophical attitude can help you to overcome even deep seated issued within your love life. It is the time to put effort into resolving anything which you and your partner have had difficulty

CAREER

December is a highly successful month for Pisces who work in industries like building, architecture, aviation, the motor industry and also clothes making or crafting. If you work with you hands or make/design something mechanical in nature you can make strides and get some recognition as well.

You will be given quite a bit of added responsibility this year especially when it comes to management and you may have to psyche yourself up before you accept, but this is an excellent chance to prove your yourself that you can move to the next level in terms of responsibility or difficulty. This is not a time when you necessarily welcome challenges, but you may have to face them as way to test your self-belief – perhaps the person giving you the new role believe in your more than you do in yourself.

Self-discipline is vital in your career as is your ability to meet deadlines and allocate your time – so draw up a schedule keep to it. You have the ability both now and in the New Year to reach a place in your career where you have far more freedom – that is freedom to create or manage people or more flexible working hours.

Pisces who are thinking of a new career may pursue something which their mother either did herself or wanted to do – although you should not fall into the trap of living out her unfulfilled dreams.

This December you have a chance not to define yourself by what you, but by how you do it – you are able to bring your idealism and concern for humanity to your work adding a meaningful dimension to what could be a 9-5 grind.